A Puppy in the Home

Of all the pets that you migh there is no doubt that the mos loyal is the dog. Its way of life i similar to that of humans that find that it was the first anima probably some 10,000 or so ye

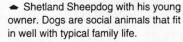

◄ Shetland Sheepdog with his young owner. Dogs are social animals that fit in well with typical family life.

◄ Neapolitan Mastiff, a rare Italian breed that can grow to 150 pounds. These puppies are a few months of age.

social animal, and fits in perfectly with family life. The members of the household are regarded by the dog as fellow pack members, the more so if the dog is acquired as a puppy.

Over the centuries dogs have been selectively bred to perform many roles, and many of the present-day breeds are physically very different from the wolves from which the first dogs were developed. However, most have retained the sterling qualities of these prime predators. The dog is happy working in a family unit, it is an excellent guard, it displays the same degree of loyalty to its family as do wolf pack members, and it easily shows its enjoyment of life when playing with

◄ The Chihuahua is the world's smallest breed.

Bulldogs originated in Great Britain and reach 55 pounds at a height of about 14 inches.

Bull Terriers are British and reach 62 pounds when fully grown. They belong to the Mastiff group and are not ferocious dogs.

family members. Within the framework of a family unit, a well-cared-for puppy can be expected to live 10-15 years, depending on the breed. In general, the smaller breeds will outlive the larger ones.

INITIAL CONSIDERATIONS

Given the tremendous array of breeds you can choose from, it certainly pays to ponder their virtues and drawbacks before going out and obtaining a puppy. If you rush this decision, you may have many years to regret the choice or be faced with the possibility of having to part with your pet a year or two down the line. Let us examine some of the major factors your family should discuss.

The most important decision is if indeed a puppy is suited to your family and your home. A puppy needs companionship. If you spend much time away from home, then the puppy will be very unhappy, so it is not the best pet to own. It will also grow up, and so you must be able to keep it from wandering off. It must be trained, regardless of its breed, so that it does not become another menace to society—there are enough of this sort of dog already. You must be a very responsible dog owner and bring it up as you would expect other people to do if they were your neighbors.

Choice of breed: Many owners select a breed because it has impressed them on TV, or because they have seen it at a dog show, or because they think it will make a super watchdog. Your puppy should suit your circumstances and not be based on those of other people. Longcoated breeds look great in the show ring, but many hours go into grooming those gorgeous coats. When your adult dog comes in covered in mud or rain you may soon wish you had selected a shortcoated breed. If you live in a very warm climate then a longcoated breed will suffer as the temperature climbs.

A large breed will cost quite a lot to feed, while any of the traditional guard breeds can become decided liabilities as they mature. Trimmed breeds, such as poodles and many terriers, will soon look unsightly if you do not have them professionally groomed, which should be done about every six to eight weeks. Some breeds, such as the large scent and gazehounds, will need a great deal of exercise. These would be a poor choice if you lived in a city and had little time for exercising.

Do not be swayed by breeds which might

◆ The Shiba Inu is a small Japanese dog (*Inu* in Japanese means *dog*). Most of the Shiba Inus weigh about 22 pounds maximum.

◀ This Labrador Retriever with a Gumabone® equipped with dental tips for the control of plaque.

◆ Two liver-nosed chocolate Poodle puppies. This is my favorite breed but they require constant grooming to look their best. Poodles come in three sizes: **Toys** are under 10 inches at the shoulder. **Miniatures** are 10-15 inches. **Standards** are over 15 inches.

currently be fashionable; these change over the years. Many of the less popular breeds can actually prove to be sounder purchases because they are not plagued by the type of breeder who is in the business for quick profits while the breed is very popular. If you wish to learn about the different breeds in greater detail, I would recommend you obtain a copy of *The Atlas of Dog Breeds of the World* or one of the other fine large books published by TFH which cover all the breeds in depth. Time spent researching the right breed for you will be time very well spent.

☛ Siberian Huskies are a popular breed that reach 60 pounds. Some have gray, ghost-like, piercing eyes.

A Wire-haired Miniature Dachshund with two pups.

The regal Borzoi is a Russian hunting breed that reaches 31 inches and 105 pounds.

Accommodation

Your puppy can be accommodated in kennels or in your home. This book is written for those who wish to have their dogs living as part of the family. This is the best way to build a close relationship with your puppy. Dogs are not solitary creatures and really do need the companionship of others– be it their own kind or that of humans.

Within your home the puppy should be given due consideration as a living being. It will want its own special place to sleep. This area should be well away from any drafts, and private enough that the puppy knows it will not be disturbed when it goes to its bed. It is especially important that young children are made aware of the fact that when the puppy goes to its resting place it must not be disturbed. If they persist in doing this then the result will almost certainly be a nervous and potentially aggressive adult dog.

TYPES OF BEDDING

There is a wide range of beds made for dogs which use a number of materials. There are bean bag types, canvas over wire-framed beds, wicker basket beds, those made of wood and those of molded plastics and fiberglass in various qualities. You can even purchase indoor traditional kennels that have been decorated in bright colors so they will blend in with your furniture. When deciding on the puppy's bed, consider the following points:

1. It should be sturdy, thus giving long life, yet comfortable.

2. It must be large enough that it will be adequate when the puppy grows to maturity.

3. It should be easy to clean. Wicker is not a good choice with this aspect in mind. Fiberglass is an excellent material because parasites can

find no places of refuge in it.

Some of the beds will come complete with cushions, while for other styles you will need to supply the cushions or simply use blankets. The latter must be changed every few days and washed so they never become a home for bugs, fleas and other unwanted visitors. Given the fact that nearly all pups will gnaw on their beds at teething time, it is perhaps worthwhile to use a cut-down stout cardboard box initially. Line it with newspapers and place a blanket on top of them. Once the puppy is past its teething period you can then purchase a nice bed which, hopefully, it will not chew.

An alternative choice to a bed would be to buy a carry crate and place a cushion or blankets in it. The advantage of the dog crate is that it enables you to restrict the pup's movement when you need to. Further, the puppy can be taken, complete with its bed, when you go on vacation, or it can be used to take the pup to the vet. It is a good all-around investment even if you purchase a separate bed. Be sure the crate is large enough for your breed when it matures. It must be able to stand upright in it and have a few inches to spare.

You may of course let your puppy sleep on your own bed with you. This should only be allowed if you intend to let the pup sleep with you when it is fully grown; otherwise, it will not understand the change in your attitude. Likewise, only let the pup sleep on chairs if this will be allowed when it is mature. It is most important that you are always consistent in your dealings with a puppy and this will ensure it grows up with a sound temperament.

◆ The Hagen Dog House for small and medium-size dogs.

The Hagen Dog House also comes with a door to keep out the rain and snow...or keep in the dog. ◆

◗ The Hagen small dog carriers come in many sizes and colors.

◗ Small dog carriers can be used for shipping dogs by air.

◗ Small dog carriers are useful for taking your dog on trips.

The Shih Tzu originated in China. *Shih Tzu* means *lion dog* in Chinese. It is a lap dog that may reach 16 pounds. They are very friendly but require constant grooming.

Whippets are fast moving dogs often used in dog racing. They are very fast, moving at 35 miles per hour. They reach 28 pounds at 22 inches in shoulder height. The dog shown here is chewing on his Nylabone Gumabone, an essential dental device for keeping dogs' teeth and gums in good condition (according to studies published in the veterinary journals).

Miniature Pinschers are a toy breed.

Choosing a Puppy

There are two aspects that this heading embraces. One is in selecting the quality of puppy to meet your needs, the other is concerned with ensuring, as much as is possible, that the pup is healthy.

THE QUALITY OF THE PUPPY

If you are interested in exhibiting your puppy when it gets older, then you will obviously need a better quality puppy than if it is to be purely a pet. The same applies if you are contemplating becoming a breeder. If the pup is simply to be a companion, then you may find that a crossbreed or mongrel will suit your needs admirably. A crossbreed is when two recognized breeds are paired, while a mongrel, or mutt, is of totally unknown ancestry.

There are virtues in each of these choices. The better the quality of the breed, the greater are your chances of winning a title. A well-bred bitch may not be good enough to take honors in the show ring but she may be a super brood bitch that can produce show winners. A purebred with some fault that would not win in the show ring, or be a good breeding proposition, will still

have all the virtues of the breed and can make a super
pet. The crossbreed combines the
virtues of its parent breeds and in some
instances may excel over either of the
parents as a working or sports dog.
Finally, the mongrel may not boast any
great lineage but the chances are it will
be a more healthy and robust dog due to
what is termed hybrid vigor. It will usually
be less able to excel in specialized roles when
compared to purebred dogs (such as gundog
work, herding, guarding and the like) but
may well be able to fulfill many roles—its
genetic makeup will give it the versatility that
might be lacking in some purebreds. It will also be
considerably less expensive to obtain. The negatives of
mongrels is that you cannot be sure what they will look
like when they grow up, or how large they might
become. The size of their paws when about 8-10 weeks
of age will give you some clues as to their eventual size,
as will the relationship of leg to back length.

▲ Dandie Dinmonts are a friendly
breed which is rarely seen except in the
show ring.

WHERE TO PURCHASE FROM

If you are looking for a top-quality puppy you should
contact an established breeder of the breed that
appeals to you. You can visit large or local dog shows,
obtain any of the doggy journals (especially those that
give show results as these will carry more breeder
advertisements), or ask at your pet shop or veterinary
clinic if they can supply any names and addresses.
Your national kennel club will give you the names of
breed clubs and these may produce yearboooks
featuring all the top breeders.

Breeders will also have a number of pet quality
puppies that they know will never make show or
breeding stock. Good pet shops may also have a

▶ The Dalmatian is an easily recognized breed which represents
the *fire dog*. From the breed's early days as a carriage dog,
firemen have adopted this breed as their own! This is a very
popular breed which reaches 55 pounds at 22 inches.

▶ Beagles are one of Americas favorite breeds. They are excellent hunters and wonderful house dogs.

◀ Bullmastiffs were used in England as guard dogs which protected grounds from poachers. They have evolved to be excellent pets that make *scary* watchdogs.

▶ The Chesapeake Bay Retriever is a hunting dog used for retrieving ducks shot down over water.

selection of pet quality purebred dogs, as well as maybe one or two crossbreeds and mongrels. Your local dog welfare agency may also have a selection of puppies that for one reason or another have been abandoned or brought in as strays. Finally, your local newspaper will always have some ads of puppies for sale and these will range from nice pups to those which are rather nondescript in terms of quality.

SELECTING A HEALTHY PUPPY

The first guide to the health of a pup is the general level of cleanliness in the place which has it for sale–be it breeder, house, or pet shop. You should not expect to see dirty conditions, uncleaned food and water dishes, or dried fecal matter lying about. These should see you looking elsewhere!

Always watch the pups as they run towards you and while they are at play. The timid ones will not be suited to a household in which there are young children. Conversely, these might be ideal for those who are themselves quiet in their manner. You can discount any pup that shows evidence of an impediment in its movements. This may be due to a simple strain through play, or it might indicate a genetic fault in the structure of the bones.

Lift up each puppy and check him over. The eyes should be bright, clear and with a decided sparkle to them. The nose should be dry to just moist. The breath should smell sweet and the teeth pure white. The upper teeth should just overlap those of the lower jaw in most breeds. Boxers, Pekingese, Bulldogs and similar breeds have undershot jaws, meaning the lower incisors protrude in front of those of the upper jaw.

The skin should be examined for any signs of parasites—fleas or lice. The former will scurry away as you brush the fur backwards, the latter are slower and gray in color. These indicate unclean conditions and a lack of attention by the owner. The fur will look healthy and there will be no bald patches in it, nor will there be any signs of swellings on the body or legs. The ears will be clean. There should be no dried fecal matter on the anus, nor should there be any signs of staining to the fur in this region. The pup should be plump and with loose skin. No bones should be apparent, which would indicate lack of food. The pads should be soft and you can check that all of the digits are correct—there are five on the front feet and four on the back. Dewclaws (found higher up on the legs) may or may not be apparent, but they are better removed in most instances as they sometimes get caught on things and tear if they are especially large and pendulous.

Avoid any pup with weeping eyes or nose, dirty and foul-smelling ears or bad breath, abrasions or swellings on its body. A pot belly (as opposed to well rounded) usually indicates worms, while a badly stained rear end may indicate very loose bowels, which in turn might suggest a problem, minor or major.

Depending on the age of the puppy it may have received temporary or permanent injections against major diseases such as hard pad and distemper. Some breeders may offer a guarantee of health but do not expect this. You should expect a veterinary health certificate with any purebred puppy, the more so if it is an expensive pup.

AGE TO PURCHASE

Breeders vary in their attitudes to this subject, some believing in retaining pups for longer than others. I would suggest that 10-12 weeks is a good age because by this time the pups should be well socialized and be confident about the world they are living in. Pups of 6-10 weeks of age will require more attention, the more so the younger they are. If you have young children, then go for the older

The Cairn Terrier is a small dog that is becoming more and more popular. ➤

The Pomeranian is a small lap dog ideal for small apartments where larger dogs might be a problem with their loud barking and large droppings.

➤ The Cardigan Welsh Corgi is a tough but very friendly short breed. It is very hardy and is one of England's favorite breeds.

puppy. Pups over 12 weeks of age are still sound purchases, depending on your situation, but obviously if you acquire a four-to-six-month-old pup you have missed out on some of its amusing ways as a young pup. This may be an advantage to some people who would rather take on a pup that is past its chewing phase, or which is required as a potential show dog.

If you are at all unsure about the health of a given pup, then it is best to pass it by. If there is one thing

These lovely Doberman Pinscher puppies will eventually reach 88 pounds at 28 inches if they are well fed. These are a natural watch dogs and one of the best for protection, too.

A Golden Retriever chewing on his Nylabone® Plaque Attacker™ to keep his teeth clean and his gums healthy.

that can really spoil your initial enjoyment, it is to find you have purchased an unwell puppy which requires costly veterinary treatment.

A family of English Setters. These are outdoor hunting dogs.

The English Springer Spaniel originated in Britain. It may reach a height of 20 inches and weigh as much as 55 pounds.

The Early Days

Once you have decided on the breed you are to purchase, and have maybe booked the puppy, it is then a good time to purchase the items you will need in readiness for its arrival. In many instances you can make do with items in your home, but most puppy owners like the new family member to have its own accessories. Those you may need are:

1. Dishes for food and water. The aluminum or crock ones will last longer but plastics are less expensive. Choose one suited to the size and breed. Long-eared breeds need narrower openings so their ears are not dangling in the dish.

2. Grooming utensils. For most breeds a double-sided comb (medium and fine), plus a stiff brush, should meet your needs. For longcoated breeds a curry or slicker brush will be beneficial.

3. Puppy collar and lead suited to the size of the puppy. These will only last a short while before you will need larger replacements of a more substantial material.

4. Small stock of food. Ask the seller what they have been feeding the puppy on and obtain some of this. It is never wise to change the diet of a newly acquired pup until it has settled into your home.

THE FIRST DAYS

Try to collect your puppy early in the day so that it has some time to settle in before its first night in its new home. When you take the pup home you will require a signed pedigree and registration form so you can transfer the pup to your name. Also needed will be any vaccination papers, a receipt, and a copy of the owner's feeding regimen. If the journey home is a long one, then do stop for breaks in quiet rest areas and be prepared for the fact that the pup may be carsick. Have a cardboard box with you which is lined with

Every dog should have an I.D. tag attached to its collar. The Hagen I.D. also reflects light, helping motorists see a dog on the road from long distances.

You need a grooming set for most breeds of dog.

Every dog needs a place in which to eat. Be sure to clean the dog's food and water dishes on a regular basis...the same as you would clean your own dishes and glasses.

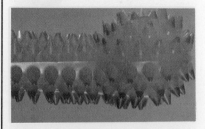

◄ A closeup of the *teeth* on the Gumabone® Plaque Attacker™. This product has the advantage of being a toy, a training device (for retrieving) and a toothbrush of sorts.

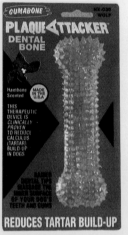

◄ The Gumabone® Plaque Attacker™ was specifically designed for reducing tartar and plaque in a dog's mouth.

Massive Plaque Attackers™ are available for larger breeds. This is a Dental Ball.

plenty of newspapers.

Once home see if the pup wants a drink of water or diluted milk and maybe a light meal. It should then be allowed to sleep if it wants to. Be very strict with children where pups are concerned. They must never be allowed to tease the pup, drag it, dangle it by its front legs, or in any other way handle it in a manner you would not want your own children handled.

A puppy can easily hurt itself in a home so be sure that there are no electrical wires trailing where it might chew on them. Be careful with anything that is hanging from tables and which the pup might jump at when playing. Irons in use can be dangerous if you leave them for a moment; the pup might pull on the cable. Open windows can cause drafts that suddenly slam doors on the pup. Other potential dangers are open fires, garden or swimming pools without protective fencing, balconies and yards or gardens which are not walled or fenced.

It is important that from the moment you obtain your puppy it is given lots of fuss. This starts the association process and the implantation of humans on the puppy.

▶ A Nylabone® or Gumabone® cannot be too large...it can only be too small. Replace all Nylabones® or Gumabones® as soon as a knuckle is chewed off.

This will be so essential in the coming weeks when its training is underway. The more the pup loves your family, the more it will want to please you.

It is very important that a puppy's life follows a regular pattern. Do not let it do things as an infant that will annoy you once it is an adult, such as sleeping on chairs, chewing old slippers, or barking at every person who comes to the home.

You can easily cure pups of bad habits but these become harder to correct if they have been encouraged when your dog is a puppy.

Feeding

The nutrition of any animal is a very complicated subject. You are therefore recommended to seek out more detailed information on this subject. Here we can look at the major aspects of feeding as applied to dogs and puppies. Dogs are prime carnivores and secondary herbivores. This means that their basic diet must be composed of meat. They will eat a limited amount of vegetable matter providing it has been heat treated in order to break down the cellulose walls of the vegetables. Unless this is done then much of it will simply pass through the pup's digestive system without nutrients being absorbed. In the wild the dog will obtain digested vegetables which are found within the gut of its prey species.

A BALANCED DIET

In order for your puppy to maintain excellent health, its diet must be balanced to include a number of crucial components.

1. Meats. These provide the basic building blocks of the pup's body. Meat is broken down in the digestive system into simple compounds. These are then rebuilt into the required tissues such as muscle, gut, brain, and so on. If the pup does not get sufficient quantity and quality of meats then its health and physique will suffer. You cannot make up in later life for any deficiencies while the dog was a puppy. Meat is essentially made up of proteins and the most usually fed types will be beef, lamb, pork, chicken, and various fish. Liver, heart and kidney are very rich in vitamins but should not be fed in large quantities as this would result in a dietary imbalance. Always try to offer a variety of meats; this will ensure no needed compounds are missing or

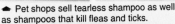

◆ Pet shops sell tearless shampoo as well as shampoos that kill fleas and ticks.

Center, This Belgian Tervuren is playing with a Gumabone® Frisbee®. This Frisbee has a bone on top so the dog can lift it off the ground when it is laying flat. **Bottom,** This Border Terrier prefers the nylon dental floss. DO NOT USE COTTON ROPES as they are organic and may rot and cause problems for your dog. Nylon ropes can be boiled and washed without weakening.

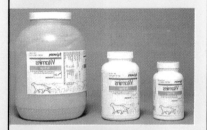

House dogs should be fed vitamins regularly.

Dog treats are fun to feed to your pet but do so sparingly.

There are hundreds of treats available. Get the best. Stay away from bulk-packed treats which do not have a manufacturer's name and address on it.

Jerky strips are a very popular treat.

given in excess.

2. Carbohydrates. These are not essential to your puppy but every dog diet will contain them because they represent the cheapest form of energy. They are found in all foods but cereal crops are especially rich in them. They are sugars of various types and when oxidized in the body they release energy which can be used to fuel the muscles. The inexpensive canned foods contain high levels of carbohydrates and these will not be adequate for the needs of a growing puppy.

3. Fats. These serve numerous functions in the body. High levels are undesirable and excess of these will be deposited as fat layers. The pup needs some fat to provide insulation, but obesity is very bad in a pup or adult dog. Fat is always found in association with meats or their by-products, such as milk, cheese, and eggs, all of which puppies really enjoy.

CHOOZ® is the edible treat from Nylabone® with the highest protein contents of any treat. It is very hard and can be softened by cooking in a microwave oven for 30-60 seconds at 400 watts.

4. Vitamins. These compounds are crucial to the health of your puppy. If you supply a balanced diet, you will have no problems. You can purchase vitamin supplements but do remember these can be very harmful in excess. If the diet is sound, then supplements will never be needed unless the puppy is recovering from an illness, in which case your vet will supply those required.

5. Minerals. These are elements needed in trace amounts, other than for calcium and phosphorus, which are important to growth and good bone development. Milk is the obvious source and this can be provided from cans (dilute condensed) or via

powdered milks prepared especially for puppies. Other minerals will be adequately supplied via the diet.

6. Water. Every animal must have regular access to water. Although it is a by-product of digesting foods, this alone will not meet the bodily needs. Always ensure water is placed fresh in a bowl each day. Depending on the moisture level of the foods given, puppies will vary in the amount of water they consume.

HOW MUCH FOOD AND HOW OFTEN?

The ratio of meat to carbohydrate should be in the order of 50/50 by weight for a puppy. The carbohydrate content should then rise steadily as the puppy matures. The adult dog will need about 30% by weight of meat to carbohydrate. Puppies are not exact machines so each will vary in its needs, depending on the following factors.

1. Size. Large breeds eat more than small ones; dogs eat more than bitches (normally).

2. Activity level. A working dog or sports dog will need much more food than will the average house pet that simply sits around the home all day.

3. Temperature. Dogs in cold climates need more food than those in warm climates. Food provides both insulation and heat, which are not needed in countries with year-round sunny climates.

4. Health. An ill puppy will eat little, but will need extra once it is recovering.

5. Individuality. Two dogs of the same breed, which live together and have the same activity level, may still vary quite a bit in their food intake. The metabolism in the one pup may be more efficient than in the other, so it needs less to retain its health.

Your guide at all times is that the puppy's weight

← This Golden Retriever has been trained to fetch his Gumabone® Giant sized dental device.

← This Beagle is working on an edible **CHOOZ**® made by Nylabone®.

15

should rise steadily, and it should always appear well muscled and in the peak of health. The amount of food per day should be based on the factors discussed. It should be divided into four meals for a 10-week-old puppy. At each meal the puppy should clear its bowl and show disinterest in further food. At this point it has eaten enough. If it eats what you give it and is looking for more, then it probably didn't get enough. You must use trial and error to establish the correct quantity and then work from this.

Two of the meals can be meat/biscuit, with the other two being milk and cereals. When the pup is about six months old you can drop one of the milk meals. When it is nine months of age discontinue one of the meat meals but add this to the remaining meat meal. If time permits, you can continue feeding two smaller meat meals, rather than one big one, and this is often much better for large dogs. It will also reduce the risk of bloat, which affects some of the heavy breeds. If you own a tall puppy, such as a Great Dane or a Wolfhound, place its dish on a raised platform so it does not have difficulty in reaching down to its food.

This Golden Retriever is chewing on a Nylabone®. Nylabone® uses the best virgin materials. Cheaper nylon bones may be made of regrind which loses it strength and may be dangerous if your dog breaks off a piece and swallows it.

The famous Russian Borzois are used for hunting. They prefer cooler climates and should not be kept in heated homes all their lives.

Baby Beagles don't need full-sized feeding bowls...or they might play in them.

This is a Brittany Spaniel. The breed originated in France. The dog will weigh 40 pounds at 20 inches.

PREPARED FOODS

Many of the proprietary foods make an excellent basis for a feeding regimen. Canned ones are the favored choice as they have a good shelf life and are very convenient. The higher priced brands are recommended as they have a better protein content. Dried foods make good standby foods and will not attract as many flies in the warmer months. Frozen foods must be well thawed before being fed. Our dogs are fed a regimen based around canned foods but with regular meals of quality meats. Biscuits are given on an ad lib sort of basis while vegetable scraps from our meals are added to the dog's plate to complete the overall balance of the feeding.

Do not feed your dog lots of sweet tidbits such as chocolates, cakes and the like, as this will not only harm its dental work but will encourage obesity. In well-cared-for homes many dogs are obese through overfeeding and lack of sufficient exercise–so do bear these points in mind.

☚ Boston Terriers are one of America's favorite breeds.

☚ A mother and puppy Cavalier King Charles Spaniel.

☚ The famous Bloodhounds which have a smelling ability 50-100 greater and keener than humans.

▶ A German Wirehaired Pointer.

☚ English Bulldogs.

Basic Training

The success or failure in training a puppy to fit into human society in a way that will make you a proud and responsible owner is determined by a number of crucial factors. The hard reality is that many pet dogs are a nuisance to neighbors, so before looking at how to train your puppy let us consider a few of the things that really go into making the anti-dog person.

1. The dog that barks all day or night when its owner is away.

2. The dog that wanders around the neighborhood, fouling gardens.

3. The dog that is allowed to chase cars or bicycles.

4. The dog that rummages through other people's trash cans.

5. The dog that jumps at visitors to a home.

6. The dog that menaces other people's pets.

7. The dog that nips people's heels or legs.

If there is one thing that will really offend people, it is to find they have a neighbor who purchases a puppy and then allows it to do any of the things stated. It totally destroys good relations. Many neighbor friends can be lost through a person's ignorance and selfishness in not attending to the basic training of their puppy.

In America certain breeds are almost unrecognizable unless they have had their ears cut. This is an unnecessary operation that is performed when the dog is very young.

The Finnish Spitz is a lovely pet dog we rarely see.

Chinese Cresteds are naturally hairless on most of their bodies.

TRAINING FACTORS

No dog is born naughty so you cannot use the excuse that your dog is stupid and does not respond to training. True, some dogs do not learn as fast as others. However, most failures are a direct reflection on the patience, character and efforts of the owners. Patterns of bad behavior commence when a dog is a puppy. To ensure these do not happen the following factors are the basics of training.

1. You must be consistent at all times with a puppy. Do not encourage an action without thinking what it could lead to.

2. You must train on the basis of affection. A puppy trained on excessive fear will develop mental problems and from these your dangerous dog emerges. Alternatively, the puppy will become a cringing sort of dog that will tell everyone, by its actions, that you are a bullying brutal sort of owner.

➥ English Setters.

◗ English Foxhound.

3. You must use canine logic, not human, when trying to understand what motivates your puppy.

4. You must appreciate that your puppy understands sound pitch and tone, not language. Many owners fail to grasp this important point.

➥ English Springer Spaniels can reach 55 pounds at 20 inches tall.

CANINE LEARNING

Your puppy learns much as you do but with one major difference. You apply logic to your decisions (even if that logic is at times difficult for others, including your puppy, to understand). This makes humans difficult to predict, but not so with your puppy. Its memory is excellent,

so its knowledge is based on recalling whether a given action proved to be to its benefit or not. Some actions are neutral on the puppy, but they may change to positives or negatives. Training is all about manipulating events such that they provide the required stimuli, be these positive or negative, so the resulting pattern of behavior is acceptable to you and other humans. Your puppy will never grow to understand that this or that is bad or good behavior, only that it results in a given reaction from yourself. A final point to be appreciated is that your puppy thinks only for the moment. It can relate to the past from its memory, but not to the future. What this means is that you cannot punish an action at the moment for a past happening. If you do, you will only confuse the puppy and make

◄ The Bichon Frise needs a lot of grooming to look good.

▲ The Tibetan Spaniel originated in China. It can reach 15 pounds at 10 inches.

◄ English Cocker Spaniels differ markedly from American Cockers. The English breed is longer in face and shorter in coat.

training even harder. The classic example of this illustrates probably the most fundamental mistake of all pet owners. The puppy has done something wrong. You see it, call the pup to you and then scold or punish it. Human logic says this seems reasonable, but it's not dog logic. You have called the pup to you and it is happy to come, now you spank it while shouting lots of words it cannot understand. As a result, the pup associates coming to you with being spanked. You then wonder why your pup seems afraid to come to you as time goes by. This you regard as disobedience, so discipline the pup even more—you have set a pattern of behavior that will make future training very much harder.

PATIENCE AND DISCIPLINE

You must have great patience with your puppy at all times, and you must be extremely fair in the way you use discipline. Never lose your temper when conducting training sessions. In most instances the pup will need no more than verbal discipline, as it wants very much to please you. Keep commands short, otherwise it will not understand what is expected–"Come, stay, sit, fetch, and down" being the most basic commands along with "no and leave" Any spanks should be restricted to light taps on the hindquarters; these will rarely be needed if you have been consistent with commands from the outset. Never commence any form of training until you have had the puppy at least two weeks. During this time your objective is to have the pup understand its name, and to feel very happy and confident in you as its friend. Encourage it to run to you often so it associates your calling it with fuss–this is an important start to all training.

Sessions, when they begin, should be short. Puppies soon get bored. Always start and end lessons on a high note so the puppy repeats that which it has already achieved at an earlier time. Success is built on success, never on failure, so the puppy must feel it is achieving something each time–even if it is that learned in earlier lessons. Do remember that your puppy can have its off days

Miniature Longhaired Dachshunds.

The faithful old friend of the world...the German Shepherd. A great watch dog, guard dog, shepherd dog and companion. ➥

The Black and Tan Coon hound is an American breed that has been developed for hunting raCOONS.

The Puli is a Hungarian shepherd dog.

The large Rhodesian Ridgeback was developed in South Africa to hunt lions.

Chow Chows originated in China.

Norwich Terrier.

The American Cocker Spaniel is one of the most popular breeds in the U.S.

just as you can, so if a lesson is not going well it is best to abandon it and end with a game. Invest in a good training manual so you can train your puppy to the most needed tasks. These are walking to heel, sitting on command, staying when told to, and keeping from barking when told to. If your puppy is given basic training (you can also join organized classes) then you will find it is highly unlikely that it will ever develop bad habits. The training will bring you and your puppy closer together.

The rare, but wonderful, Portuguese Water Dog.

Health Matters

Dogs are pretty hardy creatures and given sound management they should go through life with a minimum of problems. There are a few major diseases that they do need protection from. These are hardpad, distemper, leptospirosis, hepatitis, parvovirus, Lyme and possibly rabies. In the latter cases this will not apply to pups in Great Britain, Australia and a few other island countries. Your veterinarian will advise you on the vaccines which can be given in a combined form, though not for rabies and

➤ The Curly-coated Retriever.

◀ The English Toy Spaniel has a face that only a mother could love...but they make up for it with a charming personality.

➤ The Bouvier des Flandres is a Belgian cattle dog that reaches 88 pounds at 27 inches.

Lyme which are dealt with separately. The vaccinations are normally given when the puppy is eight or more weeks of age and a booster is given a few weeks later, thereafter annually. Even if you obtain a mongrel puppy free of charge you must still give it the protection of vaccines.

SOME COMMON PROBLEMS

In the normal day-to-day life of most pets they will sooner or later be subject to various common problems. These will include lice or fleas, worms, colds, and various minor ailments that show themselves in the face of

▶ Dogs should have their coat supplement and *Dermocare* is one of the best.

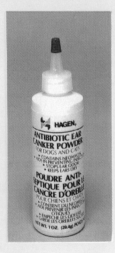

◤ A first aid cream is always handy to have around should your dog get wounded in any minor manner.

▶ You can use the Hagen Antibiotic Ear Canker Powder as a regular preventative, but ask your veterinarian for his advice if this product does not control canker.

◀ Keep your dog's ears clean with EAR-X Ear Lotion.

◤ The rarely seen but wonderful Basset Bleu de Gascogne, a French breed similar to the German Dachshund.

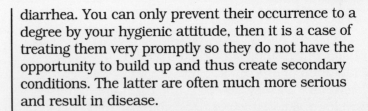

diarrhea. You can only prevent their occurrence to a degree by your hygienic attitude, then it is a case of treating them very promptly so they do not have the opportunity to build up and thus create secondary conditions. The latter are often much more serious and result in disease.

IMPORTANT "DO NOT'S"

Do not leave uneaten food in dishes. This attracts flies and quickly sours to become a breeding ground for pathogenic organisms. Water must be changed daily.

Do not use dishes once they become cracked, chipped or badly scratched (plastics) as they will harbor germs that are not easily removed during normal washing.

Do not store food in damp places, or biscuits where mice might foul them. Nor should canned goods be stored for too long a period as the vitamin content may reduce. Keep medicines and supplements out of direct sunlight—it destroys or weakens them.

Do not feed your puppy any foods that you have even the slightest doubt about in terms of its freshness.

Do not handle your puppy if you have touched other people's pets—not until you have washed your hands. Direct transfer of germs is one of the commonest causes of illness in pets.

DEALING WITH PROBLEMS

Always watch your puppy when it is urinating or defecating. Any change in the color or consistency of these might suggest a problem—very much so if you see blood or worms, or if the fecal matter becomes very liquid. In such instances contact your vet immediately. By grooming your puppy at least once a week you will notice if fleas or lice are present. These are easily eradicated with proprietary treatments from your pet shop or

The English Foxhound.

The Briard.

Smooth Miniature Dachshund.

The Boston Terrier has large eyes, which may tend to bulge and cause a problem with minor scratches and eye injuries.

vet. You must also treat the bedding and burn any loose blanketing as this will certainly house the eggs of fleas.

While grooming you can check on the pup's teeth and ears, as well as inspect the underbelly for any abrasions or swellings. If the pup looks unwell and shows no interest in its food, place it into a warm room. This will often bring about a remarkable recovery if the problem is only a minor upset. If the pup is still ill over a 24-hour period, call or take the pup to the vet immediately.

Do remember that to attempt treating a serious illness requires knowing what that illness is. Home remedies are therefore not recommended because the clinical symptoms for most major diseases are very similar. The more time you delay in contacting your vet, the more advanced the illness will become.

The Border Collie.

The Collie is larger than the Border Collie shown above.

Which Breed?

There are over 200 breeds from which you can choose your puppy–some are very popular, some are rarely seen. In size they range from the Chihuahua, the world's smallest breed, to the Irish Wolfhound, the largest. You can choose from shorthaired, medium coated and longhaired, and from those which were developed as working breeds to those which are purely lap dogs. It will be worthwhile to consider very carefully the question of size and hair length, as all too often people purchase a dog of a certain size and hair length only to find it was a bad choice once the puppy matures. Here we will look at a few breeds which collectively represent all types of dogs, and we will review them in size groups.

◀The Chihuahua originated in Mexico.

LARGE BREEDS

All of these breeds will be costly to keep in terms of their food intake–and they will invariably require quite a bit of exercise. Their size makes them more suited to country living than in small homes or city apartments. Surprisingly, the giants of the dog world are not especially renowned as guard breeds. This is because they have very docile natures so are always good where children are concerned, even though a few were kept in years gone by as sentinels and dogs of war. However, their massive size is sufficient deterrent to would-be intruders because some of them may be just as fierce as they are big!

The Irish Wolfhound, at 34in (86cm) has a medium length wiry coat that is quite easy to groom. It is a racy breed with a marvelous nature. Its colors are variable. Gentle when stroked, fierce when provoked, is an apt saying applied to this giant. Somewhat smaller and lighter, yet very similar in appearance, is the Scottish

Deerhound. If you like real elegance, then look at the Borzoi (Russian Wolfhound). Of Greyhound build, it has a beautiful medium length coat of a silky texture. Its royal looks and great speed make it an ideal country dog for those who like admiring looks from passers-by. Another member of the hound group with a royal bearing is the Afghan Hound. It has a very long coat and this helped it to gain great popularity. It also lost that status for the same reason. If you are not prepared to spend much time grooming, then you should admire, rather than own, this breed. Staying with the racers of the canine world, there is the Saluki, which is

▶Irish Wolfhound may reach 120 pounds at 34 inches.

▲The Great Dane originated in Germany not Denmark and reaches 100 pounds at 30 inches.

▲ Bullmastiff from England.

akin to an Afghan that has a smooth coat and some long hairs on the ears and tail. All of these racy breeds will attain heights of 24-30in (62-77cm). They do not eat as much as the big heavy breeds as they are quite light for their size.

The Great Dane, a German breed, is a member of the mastiff group of dogs that were developed for guarding and as war dogs. It stands up to 32in (80cm) and may weigh 100lb (45kg) or more. Its coat is short, its colors variable, and its disposition very good. It will need plenty of room to move around in. The same is true of the St. Bernard, which is slightly smaller in stature but much heavier in weight. This breed is commonly seen with

Bernese Mountain Dog from Switzerland.
◄

➥Chinese Crested coated parent with its naked offspring.

a rough coat, with dense hair, but a smoothcoated variant is available and is the better option for most people. This is a gorgeous breed, but its size, appetite and tendency to dribble much saliva may not prove to everyone's satisfaction in a household.

The Newfoundland, with its long coat, and the Mastiff, with a very short coat, are two other very heavy breeds which make fine pets if you have the space and the cash to cater for their day-to-day needs.

MEDIUM-SIZED BREEDS

Within this size range are most of the best guarding and sporting/working breeds. You should be very cautious at ever purchasing a guard breed because they do require very careful training, and an owner that has a strong will. If not, they may become very aggressive–after all, some were bred for generations to be capable of bringing a full-grown man down. However, just because a dog was born a German Shepherd or a Rottweiler does not mean it has an aggressive nature, so not all such breeds will make good guard dogs.

➥ The Schipperke is a Belgian breed (*Schipperke* means *little skipper* in Dutch).

Collies.

◄ Black Scottish Terrier.

The most popular traditional guarding breeds are the German Shepherd, the Rottweiler, the Doberman Pinscher, and the Boxer, all developed in Germany. The GSD was developed as a sheepdog but went on to gain international fame as the world's most versatile and intelligent breed. Similar to it, but much less known, are the Belgian Sheepdogs—the Tervuren, the Malinois and the Groenendael, all worthy of your further interest before making a choice.

Very popular as companion guards, especially in the USA, are a number of the Nordic breeds. These include the Alaskan Malamute, the Siberian Husky, and the Norwegian Elkhound. In recent years the Akita, developed in Japan, has become a great favorite. All of these breeds sport dense fur which must be groomed regularly. They have independent natures so tend to become closely attached to a family. In the same group are old favorites such as the Samoyed and the Chow Chow—again needing much attention to their coats.

Most of the best gundogs are of medium size and with short or easily managed coats. The Labrador and the Golden Retriever head the list in terms of

▶ The best reference book about dogs is the over-3,500-entry **CANINE LEXICON** by DePrisco and Johnson. Every dog breed (over 400) is illustrated in color with details about the breeds.

◀ Bearded Collies originated in Britain where they may reach 60 pounds at 22 inches in height.

popularity, but good all-rounders that also make great pets if you have the time to exercise them are the German Shorthaired Pointer, the Chesapeake Bay Retriever, and the Weimaraner. The setters, Irish, English and Gordon, make fine dual-purpose dogs and possess medium-length silky fur, giving them a very aristocratic look. As with all gundogs, their temperaments are usually of the very highest order, so they are ideal family dogs, especially if bred from working stock.

Within this size there is an unusual terrier, the Airedale. It is the largest well-known terrier in the world and was once a popular guard dog. It has a typical never-say-die temperament found in all terriers but makes a friendly pet. It will need its fur trimmed and this can be an added cost to bear in mind. The same is

◀ Staffordshire Bull Terrier.

Bichon Frise from France.

true of the Standard Poodle, which is a highly intelligent breed (owners claiming the most intelligent canine). It is very playful and amusing, yet was developed as a first-class gundog for retrieving from water. All of the trimmed breeds do have the advantage that they do not shed their fur, which might be an important factor to some owners.

The Border Collie is a real working breed to this day, while the Rough Collie (better known as the Lassie Collie) was bred for sheep work but rarely does this nowadays. It is an elegant dog with a lovely disposition, but its fur will need a lot of grooming. There is also a less popular Smooth Collie. The Old English Sheepdog with its wiry and dense fur is a great dog, but that fur will need a lot of time in keeping it from becoming a shaggy mess!

← English Mastiff puppy with a young Cocker Spaniel.

↓ A very popular dog breed is the Rottweiler.

SMALL BREEDS

Many of the small breeds are in the terrier group, but there are also the spaniels as well as Nordic breeds in miniature, such as the Papillon and Pomeranian. Small breeds are suited to any size home and will not burn holes in your bank account for their upkeep. They all tend to be very plucky dogs, and the larger members, such as the Pit and Staffordshire Bull Terriers, make quite formidable guard dogs that will out-perform some of their larger cousins.

Very popular in the small breeds is the profusely coated Bichon Frise. It is a perky little breed of under 12in (31cm). Within this group of toy breeds is the Havanese, the Bolognese and the Maltese, all with either flowing or long curly white coats. A tiny mastiff with a short coat is the Pug, with its wrinkled face and snub nose. If the latter type of breed appeals, then there is the heavily coated Pekingese, or maybe the Japanese Chin. The latter has longer legs and a rather less dished face–it is a super little dog. The Tibetan Spaniel is another little Oriental that is not highly popular yet has everything to recommend it as a pet.

If you like terriers, then the choice is vast. The Scottish is a long-time favorite, as are its fellow country breeds, the Cairn and the West Highland White. All will need regular trimming. If you like the Airedale but not its size, then look over the Welsh Terrier, the Lakeland, the Irish and the Wire Fox Terrier. All are similar but much smaller. The flowing coat of the Yorkshire Terrier and its diminutive size have kept it in the top ten breeds for many years, but if you would like a somewhat larger yet similar-looking breed you should check out the Silky or Australian Terrier.

Of the shortcoated breeds, the Miniature Pinscher, the Smooth Dachshunds (they come in different sizes), the Boston Terrier and the Italian Greyhound offer a range of types from the clean cut and small to the racy and the stockily built.

The spaniels comprise an interesting range of smaller breeds and two of them, the Cocker and the Cavalier King Charles, are both extremely popular in their respective homelands. The first named should not be confused with the English Cocker Spaniel, which is the original from which the very different American breed was developed. From this brief look at a few breeds you will appreciate that you are spoiled for choice in dogs. You are strongly recommended to obtain a more detailed book and look up the many other

▶ The largest and best book on dog breeds is the Wilcox and Walkowicz **THE ATLAS OF DOG BREEDS OF THE WORLD** with over 400 entries and more than 1,100 color photos.

▶ Japanese Chin.

◀ Brittany Spaniels.

Brussels Griffon.

Clumber Spaniel.

Cavalier King
Charles Spaniels.

choices, and to read about their character, size, coat type, and any special needs. The old adage, buy in haste, repent at leisure, is very apt when applied to purchasing a puppy.

English Bulldog.

West Highland White
Terrier.